THIS BOOK BELONGS TO:

_____

"It is a happy talent to know how to play."
~Ralph Waldo Emerson

David was a little boy.

He loved being a little boy and playing little boy games.

He would play go-carts with his cousin...

He would play spaceship with his sister...

He would play frisbee with his brother.

And he would also take anyone who would go with him to hike in the desert, hoping to find a treasure.

He asked himself,
"What happened to that little boy?"

Then one day, David was given a present.

The present was named Evan, and he was a little baby boy.

David and his wife Lisa watched that baby boy grow and grow, until one day Evan was a little boy himself.

Evan would say "Play with me!" so David played with Evan. They played sword-fighting, baseball, candyland, puzzles, monopoly, soccer, pro wrestling, and video games of all kinds.

Evan & David

Father and son continue to play all kinds of games together, however, David has discovered that it's not as easy to win as it used to be. Especially when they play these crazy new video games!

Ben Woolston is the published author and illustrator of the children's book "Holy Cow!" He lives with his wife and two children in Southern Nevada.